Sales & Operations Planning
RESULTS

Find, Measure, and Manage Results
Throughout Your Supply Chain

Eric J. Tinker

*P*ace Publishing Company

ISBN: 978-0-9969088-2-5

Pace Publishing Company

This book is dedicated to those who want results from their Sales & Operations Planning process and have the fortitude to rally a team to go get them.

Contents

Preface

Over the years of Sales & Operations Planning process implementation I have found that there are eight critical levers for improving and sustaining performance from this critical management planning and decision making process. These eight levers are:

- Vision
- Sponsorship
- Design
- Organizational alignment
- Reports & tools
- Enabling technology
- Results
- Change management

Nexview Consulting methodologies and training material are built around these and my more comprehensive book on S&OP will cover them in detail. I actually sat down during the summer of 2015 to write that book and this one was meant to be a chapter.

The chapter kept getting longer though, as I wanted to thoroughly cover S&OP results and the associated dimensions of results management. Thus, I decided to release this as a standalone book. It's short enough to read quickly, but still packed with information and examples.

As you might imagine, the larger book is a much more involved effort. I'm writing it while remaining active in the field of management consulting and pursuing my primary endeavor which is building a practice and boutique firm focused on S&OP and supply chain consulting. I'm not entirely sure when the larger book will come out, but it will happen.

While this book comes from an S&OP and supply chain improvement perspective, the same results management techniques can be applied to any operations improvement project and I've used them many times on manufacturing, and other types of projects as well.

The book is based on my consulting adventures over the past 20 years that have encompassed five continents and more than $500MM thus far in client benefits documented with methods described in this book. These benefits were achieved by combined consulting and client teams that I led, or had major roles on. The benefit areas mentioned in this book were often a part of these projects.

I don't take credit for the invention of the basic techniques and terms. They are used in the field of results-oriented, operations management consulting, but there is some art to this and I've written this book adding my experiences and builds on the base information.

I've also never seen a manual or other book on this in my travels thus far. The book builds on many implementations and the countless training sessions I've delivered to clients and members of my consulting teams.

As all management consultants experience, some projects are highly successful, while others end up being less than ideal for a variety of reasons. I've weaved in a few experiences where I can to illustrate successes as well as learnings.

Results tracking and management probably isn't as boring as re-reading your college statistics text, but there are a few parts of the book that get into some detail. I've balanced the detail with how to use the tools and who should be accountable for what. Change management is a critical part of this. As we know people, process, and tools all go together.

Introduction

Who can argue with results? Everyone likes them. It's what moves our companies forward, makes us feel like we did a good job and made a contribution. Not to mention, results are what advances our careers and open up bigger and better opportunities.

We're all in competition and there are winners and losers. Most of us go through our careers within one standard deviation of the mean on the distribution curve of success. Mediocrity. Results achievement can change this.

As it relates to S&OP the question is, *what can I do to get better results from my S&OP process and supply chain?* With the level of interdependencies throughout the supply chain, the question quickly becomes *how can I get others to do what I need them to do, such that we can collectively achieve a higher performance level?*

No one really improves supply chains on their own. Since it's a team effort, those leading the team need a method or system to get others to align around common goals, with accountabilities in the right places, and ways to objectively measure what can be commonly agreed upon. This is where S&OP comes in, along with a solid methodology to demonstrate improvement.

Executives lead and inspire others to achieve results and often live and die by them. It's results that typically got them where they are, and what will get them fired for lack thereof. They guide, drive, and demand, all in the pursuit of results. In large organizations, executive involvement is usually at a high level (and rightfully so). Under the layer of their experience, business acumen, and gut feel, is a layer of results quantification and ongoing measurement that makes it real and makes them and their companies successful. For business in general, we would call this accounting.

Imagine the same principle applied to a focused improvement effort or project. Like accounting, we need a layer that's tactical and detailed. We also need a way to roll up the detail to a set of project "financial statements". I hear what you are thinking. It's not always the place managers and leaders want to be. I tired of the detail myself as I strove for advancement in the field of management consulting, but someone needs to be in there, and being able to translate the detail to useful information to be communicated across levels in the organization is a useful skill. This book will help with that.

Sales & Operations Planning continues to be an area that is new for some and a work in progress for most. Teams continue to work across all aspects of the process to improve it. These include areas such as meeting content, executive sponsorship, education and alignment around what it is, making decisions more proactively, defining and managing scenarios, financial integration, as well as reporting and information systems. These are all important areas, however, the one area that will garner the most support for S&OP is demonstrating results.

S&OP as the platform for managing trade-offs and linkages for enterprise results management

I will discuss a definition for S&OP in Chapter 1, but will suggest here that results are achieved faster when the focus is placed on the higher level S&OP process, in combination with focusing improvements on the next level down supporting processes (e.g. demand planning, supply planning, procurement, distribution, etc.). It takes work at both levels to maximize success in the minimum amount of time (S&OP to coordinate the integration points and trade-offs, and local focus to execute and maximize performance in the local areas).

For example, a situation that often comes up is determining batch size. Say your planning team is working on an inventory reduction initiative and has started planning production to respond to actual demand by reducing batch size (or minimum run length in process industries) thereby reducing inventory. Sounds like a worthy endeavor and worth pursuing, right?

Yes, right up to the point this starts to increase the manufacturing complexity and cost to a degree that more than offsets the gains of the reduced batch size approach. We know that smaller batches increase changeovers, and building to exact demand could result in lumpy capacity utilization and manpower scheduling, additional scrap/transition material, reduction in throughput, variation in unit costs, and quality problems, not to mention longer lead times and more unplanned schedule changes and all the excitement that brings. So there's a balance here.

There's a lot of talk today about S&OP being used for medium and longer-term scenario planning. Thus, it would be a great place for a discussion that weighs the pros and cons of the batch size situation described above (ideally supported by a prepared business case), to get agreement on the balance that maximizes overall performance.

Another and perhaps more executive example, could be an on-shoring/off-shoring discussion that includes the trade-offs among cost, capital investment, lead time, inventory, and customer service. There are countless other scenarios we could discuss that are as varied as business itself.

Just as a quick side note, when I work with teams I always conduct workshops to pre-define scenarios for S&OP discussions. We never get them all, but it gets the team thinking and helps us illustrate to others what we should be discussing in the meetings. When the common scenarios do come up, we are primed to prepare them fully and walk into the appropriate meeting ready to shine.

Okay, back to our discussion on supply chain benefits and linkages to S&OP. The important point to recognize is that while the actual improvement and benefit measurement occurs at the lower supporting process level, it's S&OP that provides the needed integration, prioritization, and visibility to focus the cross-functional team effort and maximize the total success.

The process also communicates and educates the various parties on the totality of the situation. If you've spent a career in Sales, it just isn't your background or perhaps priority to worry about batch sizes, changeovers, or excess inventory, especially when you're incented on sales volume. Similarly, if you've spent a career in manufacturing, it's not your priority to accommodate more products or customer order changes, especially if you're incented on throughput and unit cost.

S&OP is the brain that processes all the nerve impulses to arrive at an enterprise decision, and the skeleton that keeps the muscles from going in different directions. As we deep dive into supply chain benefit areas and tactics for managing in this book, let's not forget about the brain and skeleton in the background. Like our own bodies and minds being a means for us to contribute something productive, so too is S&OP. In the end, it's just a means to get results. Lose your focus on results and linkages between results and S&OP, and it will be seen by many as a time drain.

I'll spend the majority of the time talking about measuring benefits for improvement initiatives, but let's not forget results management for the ongoing management of the business too. I'm talking about key performance indicators (KPIs) here. For S&OP, this means a layered system of KPIs managed throughout the component meetings. I'll address methods for KPI management throughout.

If you're at the 50,000 ft. level, this book will help you understand what needs to be done to measure results, hopefully provide a little appreciation for what's under the hood, the resources to allocate, and the right questions to ask. You may only want to skim some of the more detailed sections.

You know that your executive leadership, strategy, and experience will always be important, but without the tactics executed on the front line, a great strategy and all your experience won't matter.

For the project manager or person on the front line, the trick is to understand enough detail to make it happen, while implementing a system that quickly transforms the detail to an executive level summary. This book will give you enough knowledge to build a comprehensive results management system and roll the detail up for a group of executives. I'll discuss terms, tools, and techniques that have been used to manage large change projects.

All examples contained in the figures and tables are hypothetical, but representative. When we talk about quantifying S&OP and supply chain results, there are some nuts and bolts that need to be fastened together. The intent of this book is to provide the wrench and some guidelines for using it.

Note

Some spreadsheets as marked are available for download at:

http://nexviewconsulting.com/results-ebook-l-booklinks/

ONE

S&OP Checkpoint

The intent of this book is to provide guidance for achieving business results through S&OP, as opposed to emphasizing what it is and how to implement it. The next book will include that, however, I'll provide a brief overview to get us going on the same page. Throughout the book, I'll also occasionally make a reference to a particular S&OP component meeting and I want those references to be clear.

What's in a name?

Quickly, let's get the definitional thing out of the way. In this book, S&OP will refer to the management level, product family level, cross-functional planning and decision making process that integrates a company. Some may call it Integrated Business Planning, Executive S&OP, Sales Inventory Operations Planning, or other names.

In this book, S&OP does not refer to all supporting supply chain planning (e.g. demand planning, supply planning, etc.) and execution processes as some mistakenly include. In fact, this confusion has led to the other names for the process in an attempt to differentiate it or market it in some new way. In any one company, it really doesn't matter what you call it as long as you have the higher level planning and decision making process that links the strategy with the lower level planning and execution.

There are APICS and other definitions out there. I'm certainly not saying any of these are wrong. I just made up my own definition to emphasize points of my methodology.

Here it is:

S&OP is management's vehicle for communication, performance management, and intermediate term decision making related to integrating, financial, sales, and operational planning to meet company objectives.

The definition isn't meant to exclude other functions like engineering for things like new product development, or HR for things like manpower planning. It depends on the individual company situation. The definition above also calls out functions that may not apply in all industries.

Take upstream oil & gas for example (the exploration, drilling, and production of crude oil and other hydrocarbons), where my company has adapted the base principles to that very different value chain. In this part of the oil & gas industry, "Sales" is primarily an accounting transaction and my clients here didn't like that word to be connected with this process. No problem. Just change it to fit the culture.

S&OP is gaining momentum in other non-manufacturing industries as well (e.g. service-based). After all, don't all companies have customers to satisfy, a need to plan resources to meet market requirements, and integrate financial planning? Don't get too hung up on my or someone else's definition, but make sure your definition aligns with a vision that is appropriate for your application. Use first principles and common sense.

Open your mind on the design

I'd like to emphasize that the process and meetings that make up S&OP aren't standard. There is certainly what's common, and we can call this "best practice", but best practice doesn't mean it's best for you. The point I'm making is that each business has its own needs and best practice is a great place to start, but it needs to be tailored to each application.

Here's an extreme example. Consider an S&OP process without a demand review, three supply reviews, a "marketing and infrastructure review", and an integrated meeting across functions. Wow – that looks different, how can that be right? I've just described a design that has been used in upstream oil and gas. It fits the company's value chain and what I call S&OP first principles.

By first principles I mean that the design needs to align with the way the business is managed, organized, reports financially, and maintains a supporting data structure. As we know, these things often aren't in perfect alignment, and an S&OP effort is a chance to bring them together. We know that data structure one is frequently a weak point. First principles would also include the bullet points in the next section. None of these things are tied to any particular S&OP meeting structure.

The traditional S&OP components and meeting flow

S&OP is a series of meetings, typically held monthly, that bring together the sales, operating, and financial plans, and functions of a company. These plans and the discussions around them are at a product family level over a rolling planning horizon that is typically 12-24+ months in duration. The length of the planning horizon is driven by the longest lead item and the horizon required for financial planning at the product family level.

Some characteristics and benefits of S&OP include:

- Consistent plans used throughout the organization
- A structured collaborative framework that provides clear accountability for the various components and results of the underlying processes
- Led by senior management
- Exception-based discussions
- Management of financial gaps while there is still time to do something about it
- Alignment of discussion and decisions across functions that fit with the strategic direction of the company
- Business performance management across the enterprise
- Results typically delivered through focused concentration in the underlying planning processes or supply chain execution
- Platform for continuous improvement in the company
- Leadership development and improved teamwork in the company

In a manufacturing environment, the monthly S&OP cycle is typically comprised of the following components:

- **Portfolio Review** – This meeting is especially important for those companies with many SKUs or rapidly changing product portfolios. The objectives are to discuss major product introductions and discontinuances, and examine the fit of the product portfolio with company goals. The meeting ensures changes to the product portfolio are coordinated with demand management and the rest of the supply chain. Any concerns are recorded and discussed later in the process. The owner of this review is often a Vice President of Marketing.

- **Demand Review (or Consensus)** - This is a meeting to review demand inputs from various parties, achieve consensus, and confirm the unconstrained demand at the product family level. It is the culminating step in the demand planning process. Teams also discuss plans to close sales gaps relative to financial or budget commitments. Production or other concerns are recorded as issues to be resolved later in the process. This meeting is often owned by a Vice President of Sales.

- **Supply Review (or Consensus)** – This meeting is the culminating step in the supply planning process and is used to confirm the supply plan to meet the unconstrained demand plan provided from the Demand Review. As necessary, supply constraints are identified and noted as exceptions to be discussed later in the process. This meeting is often owned by a Vice President of Operations.

- **Pre-S&OP** - This is the meeting where the rolling 12-24+ monthly plan comes together and where exceptions are resolved across functions. The plan is usually a consolidated view of sales, production, and inventory by month on a volume and dollar/currency basis (or orders, production, and backlog in make-to-order environments). Analysis of exceptions, alternatives, scenarios, and financial implications is completed prior to this meeting so the issues can be dealt with effectively during the meeting.

- **Executive S&OP** – This meeting is held with the top management of the company (or division in larger corporations). This meeting quickly confirms the overall plan approved in pre-S&OP, but it is rolled up to the company or division level. It also addresses decisions that require executive involvement due to their nature or financial magnitude. The meeting is owned by the CEO or General Manager and is often worked into a monthly executive business review.

After the financial close and when data become available, the S&OP component meetings are typically spaced about one week apart. It's important that there be enough time between the meetings for the outputs of one to be used effectively as the inputs to the next.

You can see that to effectively distribute the meetings throughout the month, your accounting close must happen within a few days of month end. Companies with process gaps here will fundamentally struggle with S&OP and may have to deal with lagging information and/or aspects of a process that are not integrated with financial planning.

I've often worked with clients who are in this situation, and there are ways to still make the process meaningful while the closing process cycle time is brought in line with current standards. The other thing to remember is that S&OP isn't a "this month/next month" discussion, but it's nice to know where we are right now to help with the forward discussion, especially if there are gaps.

From the description above, and many of the models out there, it might be easy to think of S&OP as a linear process. I recommend not thinking of it that way because when one component within the cycle is completed, it's time to start thinking about the underlying process and meeting for the next cycle. I also draw pre-S&OP in the middle because it is the component that links the others together as the full plan comes together and when there is a cross-functional issue to resolve (prior to elevating the issue to executive S&OP if necessary).

Figure 1.1 The Continuous S&OP Process

As S&OP contains elements of both strategy and tactics, the component meetings must be integrated with the overall executive management meeting structure above it, and the more frequent tactical meetings below.

Takeaways from Chapter 1 – S&OP Checkpoint

- S&OP is the executive level cross-functional planning & decision making process, not everything supply chain planning
- The S&OP design, your organization structure, underlying data structure, financial reporting structure, and the way you manage the business all need to be synchronized
- Recognize and start with best practices, but create a design that makes sense for your business
- S&OP is a continuous process

TWO
Types of Results

The most powerful change management technique I know of is achieving and communicating results. Results are hard to argue with. For S&OP to be successful, it needs to be very clear that while it is a good idea, and will get people to work to a common plan and communicate better, it is above all else a vehicle for tangible results.

Definition of results

I define results simply as the *visible evidence of change*. Results are visible to a group of stakeholders. They can be demonstrated. Conceptually it's pretty simple, reality is usually a different story.

Intangible results

Considering the definition above, I think it's okay to talk briefly talk about intangible results. These are outcomes that are usually subjective and largely based on perception. I'm not saying that they aren't important, they are. I'm talking about things like:

- Improved teamwork
- Improved communication
- Increased learning
- Leadership development

- Less fire-fighting
- Culture change

Yes – there are ways to measure these things to some extent, but those measures are most likely measures of perception rather than hard number fact. Here are some data from a recent survey of peoples' perceptions.

Figure 2.1 Intangible Results from S&OP

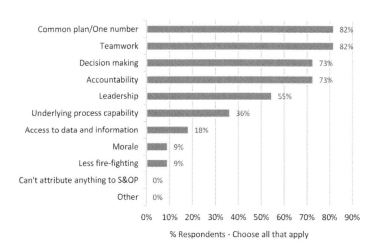

Source: Nexview Consulting Survey, 2014

Is S&OP maturity progress a result?

S&OP at most companies is a work in progress. There are lots of things to work on such as the design, the quality of the discussion, engagement of various parties, degree of focus on longer-term/more strategic items, or perhaps information systems that will improve analytical capability to model scenarios and provide decision support.

Few are proficient in all of these and other areas that would constitute a set of best practices. A maturity system usually entails laying out a path to achieve varying degrees of best practices over time. A question to ask is whether or not progress on S&OP maturity criteria is a form of results?

Let's make a distinction. We've been talking about results in terms of results for the *business*, not for the S&OP process itself. Progressing the process to a higher level of maturity should affect the business results though, so I'll say that S&OP maturity is a valid measure and can be talked about as a form of result. Note though that I've covered this point in the intangible section. Indirect could be another term we could use. "Maturity results" won't cut it alone though, we need to impact the business.

Business results need to be shown in conjunction with S&OP maturity or what's the point? It is helpful to define maturity characteristics and plot your course over time. It will help educate, align, and set expectations across the team. Some of the terminology and approaches we'll discuss in this book can be applied to measuring maturity too. I'll discuss more about maturity systems in the next book, thus will leave it for now.

Tangible results

Tangible results are objective operational and financial measurements. They can be agreed on consistently across a stakeholder group. Operational metrics should be linked to financial metrics that have traceability to financial statements. While the intangible results are important and add value, if the tangible results aren't there, the intangible ones won't matter in the long run. Achieving tangible results is not easy though. If it were, we'd all be CEOs of companies (for those of us who want that anyway).

Management of Key Performance Indicators

"How about KPIs, we have a scorecard, isn't that good enough?"

As I've mentioned, KPIs are more for the ongoing management of the business and as such need to be integrated throughout the business. Once again, I'll take the S&OP and supply chain perspective, but the concepts apply to all areas of the business.

Think of a system of KPIs like a pyramid. The individual bricks (or KPIs) are linked and build upon each other. KPIs at the top of the pyramid link to company strategy and critical success factors. As we move down the pyramid, higher level KPIs are broken down into components for accountability distribution and management across the organization.

The top level KPI targets drive expectations downward, while results of lower level KPIs serve as leading indicators for those above. Perhaps not every KPI has perfect linkages above and below it, but you should look for this and challenge the need for KPIs that don't seem to link.

As S&OP sits between business strategy and business execution, related KPIs should reflect this too. Thus, KPIs are linked to higher level business KPIs above (e.g. Return on Capital or Revenue) and are linked to the process level KPIs below (e.g. forecast error, inventory turns), which are in turn linked to even more tactical KPIs below that (e.g. number of sales meetings or inventory levels).

Figure 2.2 KPI Pyramid

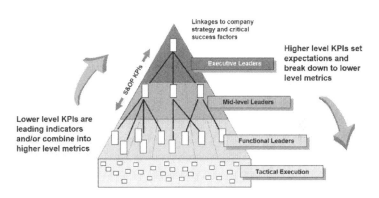

As you map KPIs to your system of S&OP meetings and seek to link them in a pyramid fashion, you may find the same KPIs in multiple meetings, but the level of the KPI or view of it should be different across the meetings. For example in a demand review, you may look at forecast error by sales territory or customer, but in pre-S&OP you may look at it by product family or regionally, and in the executive meeting you may discuss it at a company level.

KPIs/metrics are typically tangible quantities. I say typically because some may have measures on process compliance (e.g. meetings attended) and I'm not talking about things like this.

Everyone has a scorecard. Several with too many KPIs on them. While many scorecards can be improved upon, the management issues are typically around how the KPIs are used, how gaps are addressed, lack of root cause analysis, and lack of actions to address root causes. Two questions I always try to get meeting leaders to ask are:

1. *When will we be back on track?*

2. *What do we need to do to make sure it doesn't happen again?*

Perhaps you have an S&OP process in place and you just need to improve the focus and management of your metrics so you can move them. That's okay and certainly a good starting point. I'd offer though that you should review your scorecard for the items discussed in Chapter 4 and include those items if they are missing.

The most basic point to emphasize for KPI management is that you measure and manage *something*, and that something produces a business result. S&OP takes work and if you don't make progress on your measurements, your process could very well lose steam. The tools and techniques in this book will give you some ideas for where to look for results and will help you mechanize a system to manage them on an ongoing basis.

Reasons why many efforts do not show tangible results

Think of all the effort being expended on improvement initiatives underway right now across the world. The majority of them will never show any tangible results. Here's a few reasons why.

Table 2.1 Common Reasons Why Improvement Programs Show No Tangible Results

PEOPLE RELATED	PROCESS RELATED
1. Lack of consistent management commitment	10. Jumped into the project without first conducting an assessment and committing to improvement targets
2. Insufficient resources allocated to the project	
3. Lack of a sense of urgency	
4. Changing priorities in the business	11. Didn't define a baseline from which to measure improvement
5. Impacts attributed to factors other than the project	12. Didn't link daily activities to levers that drive results
6. Couldn't agree on benefit areas, magnitude, or time to achieve	13. Difficulty in quantifying under changing business conditions
7. Couldn't agree on tracking methodology	14. Inability to influence integration points
8. Afraid to commit to results	15. Resources not allocated to track
9. Executive in charge knew the project was just needed, quantifying results isn't necessary in his/her mind	16. Just didn't do it

CASE STUDY – LESSON LEARNED

Some years ago, I was involved in a consulting project with a global consumer products company. I was hired by a consulting firm after the project was sold, set-up, and underway. An assessment had not been completed, but there was a loose benefits case associated with our S&OP project. Despite trying to raise the visibility of the results case, I didn't have all the necessary positioning as I was transitioning in.

I compromised on results management and the positioning thing amidst the many other things going on, and to keep the peace in my new situation. Later in the project, we struggled with schedule due to IT delays brought about by late acceptance of infrastructure gaps to support S&OP, stop-gap custom tool development, as well as some IT-related dynamics/change management issues that are common in large organizations.

As our project was nearing the end of its budget allocation, a large corporate-wide ERP project was beginning and the remaining parts of our project were absorbed by the larger project. The client lost time achieving results and had to repeat some things. Had our project emphasized a visible and jointly committed results case, the client may have set a higher priority on results timing and continued with an integrated effort to achieve results faster. We did many good things on that project that helped them, but the parts about a lack of measured results and portions of our effort becoming redundant/usurped will always bother me.

The rest of our discussion will focus on getting tangible results, let's get after it.

Takeaways from Chapter 2 – Types of Results

- Intangible results are important, but it's the tangible ones that make or break things.
- Most improvement programs don't show results for many reasons.

- KPIs are a great place to start, but often come up short in the way they are managed.
- Lose your focus on tangible results and you could lose your project.

THREE

Identifying and Quantifying Your Results Case

Tangible results are what turn good ideas into "We gotta have this and will dedicate resources and ongoing effort to it." There are lots of good ideas around competing for resources and attention. If results are measured and demonstrated, people pay attention and devote energy to it. For maximum impact and support, your project and/or process should be linked to improvements in operational and financial metrics.

S&OP in and of itself will produce results, however, as it's an overarching leadership process, results can be accelerated by focusing effort in the supporting planning and executional supply chain processes. With all the moving parts in a company, it's also easier to trace specific improvements when they are linked to improvements in processes below the S&OP layer. Best results are achieved when S&OP manages results areas and focused improvement efforts address tactical areas.

Consider Figure 3.1 that shows supporting S&OP processes, a non-exhaustive list of associated KPIs, and familiar financial metrics. It's a high-level chart, but the point is that S&OP is the management system that coordinates these processes and associated result areas. As you think about tracking results connected with the process, think about the underlying processes, the associated operating metrics, and how they translate to financial impact.

Potential benefit areas

In general, the inefficiencies at the front of the supply chain result in waste downstream. For example, gaps in forecasting can result in the wrong inventory and expedited freight. You very well could have gaps that are local to the specific processes shown above, but the largest benefits can be achieved through an integrated improvement approach.

Table 3.1 is a summary of various benefit areas throughout the business that can be addressed locally as well as coordinated and managed through S&OP. Your opportunities will naturally depend upon your industry and specific situation. I'm sure there are others that I've forgotten or not thought of. Hopefully, this table and the pages that follow can be a starting point to generate some ideas for your situation.

Information systems

I've tossed in some IT acronyms in the table above as levers (e.g. MRP, DRP) or referred to "system settings", but haven't talked too much about enabling information technology. For this discussion and purposes of this book, I've assumed that the company of interest has an "average" level of IT enablement capability. This means that they can complete supply chain planning, execute transactions, generate reports and results of operations, as well as generate KPI scorecards.

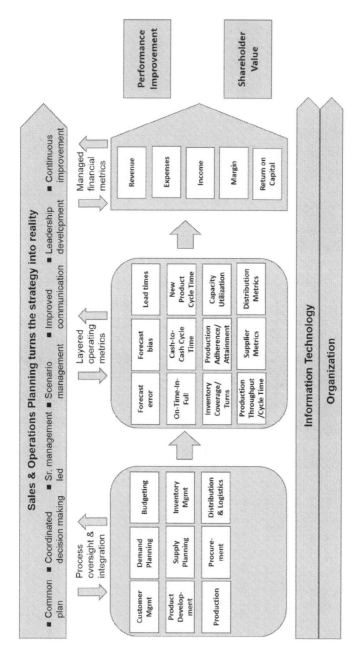

Figure 3.1 Benefit Linkages in the Supply Chain

Table 3.1 Benefit Areas That Can Be Managed Through S&OP		
Company Area	**Benefit**	**Operational Levers**
Sales	▪ Increased sales	▪ Improved on-time-in-full ▪ Reduced lead times ▪ Improved promotions management ▪ Reduced stock outs through improved inventory and demand management ▪ Improved pricing policies and management
Product Development/M anagement	▪ Increased sales	▪ Improved demand and inventory management ▪ Reduced new product development cycle time ▪ Improved stage gate process ▪ Product portfolio management
Procurement	▪ Spend reduction ▪ Transaction efficiency	▪ Strategic sourcing techniques ▪ Supplier consolidation ▪ Alliance management and reduced out-of-alliance spend ▪ Bid process for select items/services/commodity groups ▪ Supplier management techniques ▪ Transaction process improvement/reduction ▪ Outsourcing ▪ Organizational right-sizing ▪ IT improvement
Manufacturing	▪ Reduced schedule interrup-tions/ changes (cost) ▪ Reduced overtime (cost)	▪ Root cause analysis ▪ Customer segmentation and service levels ▪ Time fence management ▪ Lead time management ▪ Inventory and demand management ▪ Shop floor material control and flow ▪ Outsourcing
Inventory	▪ Right items in the right places at the right times	▪ Demand management ▪ Delayed differentiation ▪ Defined make-to-order vs. make-to-stock strategies

Table 3.1 Benefit Areas That Can Be Managed Through S&OP		
		■ Stock point rationalization ■ Improve system settings (e.g. reorder points, min/max, and safety stocks) ■ Statistical analysis ■ Improved DRP use ■ Use of CPFR ■ Consigned inventory programs with suppliers ■ Manage to targets ■ Production quantity reviews (production pegged to demand) ■ Lean techniques for WIP ■ Shop floor material control and flow ■ ABC classifications ■ Cycle counts ■ Review MRP settings and use ■ Trade-offs between holding costs and volume purchase savings on raw material (EOQ) ■ Agreed write-down and disposal policies (EBIT trade-off here)
Distribution & Logistics	■ Reduced warehouse costs ■ Reduced transportation costs	■ Stock point rationalization ■ Trade-offs among holding costs, service levels, operating expenses understood (i.e. network optimization model) ■ 3PL partners/outsource ■ Manage and reduce premium freight ■ Reduce shipments between stock points ■ Reduce non-nearest shipments ■ Improve truck utilization ■ Improved scheduling, routing, and backhaul management ■ Transportation mode optimization ■ Railcar fleet optimization ■ Reduced demurrage ■ Freight sourcing and preferred carrier programs ■ Freight invoicing audits

Table 3.1 Benefit Areas That Can Be Managed Through S&OP		
Organization	■ Right-sized organization ■ Increased organizational capacity ■ Reduced planning cycle time	■ Modern organizational structure ■ Consolidate duplicate functions/activities ■ Improved skillsets ■ Competitive compensation and advancement opportunities

If your situation is different, you should establish this capability perhaps while you are applying some of the short-term techniques described below. If your company isn't committed to supporting processes with current tools that provide improved analytical capability, your company is falling behind in organizational capability, and you are falling behind as a professional. You might figure that into your longer-term career planning.

Short-term and longer-term benefits

As you look at the items in Table 3.1, you may be thinking about what can be achieved in the short-term vs. what is going to take a longer, more integrated approach. Supply chain benefits typically have short-term and longer-term benefit realization potential. Take inventory right-sizing for example. Short-term improvements may involve setting targets based on the statistics of the current situation, updating the system settings, managing to those targets, scrutinizing the production schedule, and improving controls around ordering raw material.

Longer-term improvements might include things such as improving forecasting, smoothing demand if possible, improving collaboration with key customers, consolidating stock points, etc. Differentiating short and long-term actions that will drive benefits will become important as you put your benefit cases on a timeline. We'll discuss more about timelines later in the chapter.

CASE STUDY – A PIECE OF HISTORY THAT STILL WORKS

The Hawthorne Effect

The Hawthorne Effect is named after a series of labor productivity studies that were conducted by a group of Harvard industrial psychologists between 1924 and 1932 in Western Electric's Hawthorne plant near Chicago. While academics and others have gone back and forth on the conclusions of the studies over the years, the Hawthorne Effect refers to the notion that the mere attention to a particular item will result in an improvement in performance or productivity. Operations improvement consultants will sometimes use the term and often believe that some level of short-term improvement is possible as described above.

I've seen this phenomenon produce some short-term results in some situations. While it is certainly no substitute for the techniques to make significant and sustainable performance improvements, if it provides a little boost at the beginning of a project, we'll take it!

Comments on specific benefit areas

In this section I'll give you a few comments and tips on the benefit areas mentioned in Table 3.1 above. They aren't exhaustive, but here are a few experiences and things to watch for.

Sales and margins

Sales and margin benefits can often be the largest of all benefits listed in the table. They can also be the most difficult to achieve, and it can be difficult to separate market conditions and effects from project activities. Thus diligent definition and tracking mechanisms will be required.

Customer and market input can sometimes be helpful to help quantify. For example, what levels of improvement in on-time-in-full and/or lead time reductions will generate additional sales? How many stock outs did we have that resulted in lost sales?

What was the true demand requested vs. what was actually shipped? What was the lift associated with a particular promotion and should we do more at the expense of margin erosion? Do we have a good handle on price elasticity and our true profitability at the product and customer level?

Answers to questions like these along with the locations of the socks that disappeared in the dryer are among the secrets of the universe. These items take a bit more digging to track (perhaps estimate), but analytics are getting better all the time and it is possible. Don't forget too that increased revenue is certainly important and nice, but it's the margin that's the benefit.

Product development and product portfolio management

Achieving benefits here often comes down to cycle time compression in developing new products and effectiveness in getting them into the supply chain and market. Picking the ones that will have high demand sure helps too.

The other part of this is managing the ongoing product portfolio which requires a good understanding of revenue and margin at the product level. The true profitability isn't always easy to get if you want to get into the activity based costing side and most companies don't have good visibility of this. Many companies with tens of thousands of SKUs don't actively manage product portfolios and this can unnecessarily drive complexity and hidden cost.

Understanding this can not only lead to potential cost reduction, but also lead to significant increases in profit. The 80/20 rule applies in most situations and is an easy chart to draw if you have revenue and profitability data at the product level.

By 80/20, I mean that eighty percent of the revenue and/or margin comes from 20% of the products. Often this ratio is even worse making a case that cost and complexity can be taken out by trimming the product portfolio.

Of course there are other considerations such as customers' desires for one-stop-shopping and perceived growth potential which may or may not have merit. If the rate of new product introductions exceeds the rate of product discontinuances, the added growth needs to more than compensate for the added complexity. It sounds obvious, but in practice many companies don't quantify the added complexity and should be trimming their product portfolios.

Discontinuing products can become very emotional with commercial organizations, so it's good to have some of that 80/20 style data behind it. If you take products out and don't ramp up the volume of what remains (or cut overhead proportionally), you'll have overhead absorption issues that will drive unit costs up which could cloud decision making. The trick is obviously to have demand substitute or new and more profitable products.

Procurement

I like procurement benefits and improvement efforts because there always seems to be improvement potential here. There are usually areas that haven't been sourced in a while and are ripe for looking at again. While no benefit area is easy to get, procurement benefit are more defined and easier to get than generating sales or right-sizing inventory. My projects have never failed in this area (knock-on-wood), which isn't true of all benefit categories.

Procurement professionals are typically very guarded about signing up for these benefits. After all they've poured their hearts and souls into getting the best deals and now it looks like they've not been doing their jobs. Many times I've heard things like "I've been working in this area for 10 years and in 3 weeks, you come in and tell me that I can get a better deal, I don't think so!" More on this overall point in Chapter 6.

Watch out for market effects here (e.g. rising commodity prices), don't ignore indirect spend and services, and make sure you understand what part of the spend is already under long-term agreement. Knocking off a few percent on price on large volume items can result in huge savings. Whole consulting firms and empires have been built on just this.

Manufacturing

For manufacturing, I'll limit our discussion to the more integrated benefits connected with S&OP. Thus I've not listed improvements strictly for plant operations (e.g. reduced scrap). The efforts in production scheduling are frequently around trying to stabilize the schedule which often requires definition of frozen periods and which customers we'll break the schedule for (i.e. customer segmentation).

We also look at product sequencing/wheels, batch sizes, and master data/settings in the scheduling system. This would include things like capacity and utilization settings, routings, cycle times, and bills of materials. This piece is clearly tightly integrated with a review of the MRP raw material planning processes.

We look at production attainment and schedule adherence, and determine root causes for deviations. They often trace back to schedule changes, raw material delays, or more operational items such as maintenance, quality, perhaps staffing (but this should be fixable in the short-term).

On the operations side you hear terms and techniques such as production loss accounting, root cause analysis, short interval controls, preventive maintenance programs, and tactically focused KPI targets and meetings, and of course application of lean/pull systems and all that they entail.

For supply chain/S&OP items, I think it's okay to bring in some of the summary level metrics into the supply review discussions, especially those related to future planning quantities. For S&OP, it's important that the discussion stick to the S&OP horizon and not the tactical production components.

The tactical items are important, but should be addressed in as part of the production management system. Thus, there's an interface/delineation between supply review and the tactical production meetings. Examples of good S&OP-level metrics might be things such as capacity utilization, production schedule adherence, and overtime over the month. The tactical production meetings could look at these metrics on a more frequent basis.

Inventory

Whole books are written on just this, so I'll only say a couple things and refer you back to Table 3.1 for some summary bullet points. The sins of supply chain often end up inventory and there are many levers here. Several of the levers integrate with improved network inventory management, planning, IT settings, and customer management policies. If you don't have operational and statistical reasoning behind your inventory targets, finance will just tell you what they are based on financial constraints, wish list, or edict. Inventory is probably the toughest benefit to get in my experience. Ironically as much as people like to talk about it, in the end, most situations are driven by the P&L, sometimes at the expense of optimizing inventory.

Distribution & logistics

This is another popular area because it is typically a large bucket of supply chain cost. Similar to procurement, careers and firms can be built on this too (which is fine). There's a procurement aspect of this (freight sourcing) and spend management techniques apply here. There's also an operational component to this and opportunities for savings often result from gaps in upstream planning and inventory management. Obviously fuel prices figure prominently into these costs. More on this point later.

It's now much rarer for companies to have their own truck fleets, but it still happens or is a mix, especially in some parts of the world. If you have your own fleet, ask yourself if your brand really warrants the extra cost and management of your own fleet. Do your painted trucks really generate more sales? Unless you're a trucking company, if you're still managing a fleet and employing truck drivers, you should review the outsourcing option.

The biggest benefits in warehousing are usually associated with eliminating them. If you have 5 in the United States you can get anywhere within 1-2 days. There are a variety of reasons why companies have more, not all of which are driven by science. The science is driven by trading off operating expenses and inventory costs with customer requirements (lead time) or perhaps by specific product handling requirements (such as those for some applications in life sciences).

The other part of the warehousing benefit is in improving operations within the warehouse itself in terms of staff, automation/tracking, layout, and inventory management efficiencies. Warehousing has been another area for outsourcing that's been popular for the last few decades. Third party logistics (3PLs) providers that provide transportation and warehousing has been a great solution for many companies.

I have found that operating expenses associated with warehouses sometimes often aren't as large as you'd think. You need to check the numbers to see if it's worth it, but don't forget, a reduction in complexity is good too!

For companies with railcar fleets, the opportunity here is improving the utilization (i.e. railcar turns), by managing the parts of the railcar cycle that are most impactable (i.e. when the railcar isn't moving). Higher railcars turns (trips per year), means more trips for the same production with a smaller fleet.

Less cars obviously means less cost. There is a secondary market for "swapping cars" amongst parties that need cars for short durations or would like to re-lease cars they may not need. This is a cottage industry.

Reducing demurrage charges may be an opportunity if you pay these (common in trucking, tanker railcars, and ocean). Gaps in planning & scheduling are usually the culprit. If your customers are hanging on to your hopper railcars for too long and you want to charge them demurrage, I've found it's often not as easy to charge for or collect, even when it's in the customer contracts. I've had sales leaders balk at this one when it comes time to enforce demurrage collection. Better put the accountability in the right place when signing up for this one.

Organization

Consultants often speak about "creating organizational capacity." We look for things like outdated structures, too many organizational layers, fragmented or inconsistent reporting relationships, duplication of tasks, or roles with too many tasks (e.g. "the supply chain guy"), people dependent processes, lack of analytical capability, and gaps in roles & responsibility definition.

One of my favorite studies is called an Activity Dispersion Analysis where we get peoples' perceptions as to who does what and is accountable for various supply chain tasks. Results are often all over the place, which indicates that the group does not have a common understanding of roles & responsibilities. Conversely, if you've got that person who can't take a vacation without on-time-in-full taking a hit then you have some organizational work to do as well.

Most larger organizations have gone to centralized "center of excellence" structures. Perhaps a buzzword, but the structure is meant to build a tightly integrated team around integrated processes (e.g. demand and supply planning or order fulfillment). The idea is to build uniform processes and capabilities using best practices, common tools, and consistent leadership direction. The best way to do that is through a single reporting structure and capability expectation.

This doesn't mean that a team member couldn't specialize and have dotted line relationships to business units or plant locations. For example, a demand manager could report to a director of supply chain, but do the demand planning for Asia and have a dotted line to that business unit general manager.

It also usually makes sense to separate the longer-term S&OP level planning tasks (demand planning, supply planning) from the daily executional tasks (e.g. production scheduling, logistics scheduling). Smaller organizations may not always have this luxury.

Without distinct short-term execution and medium to longer-term mindsets and processes, when executional folks have key roles in S&OP meetings, it's unlikely that their discussion will cover a best practice level or horizon and the execs will just check-out and run the company somewhere else.

Creating organizational capacity is a real benefit. The question becomes, how do you want to cash the check? Does that mean a hiring avoidance in the future, adding missing capability (e.g. analytical or improved used of IT), or does it mean letting people go? I don't need to tell you how sensitive this last one can be. Better spell it out and get sign-off on something called a baseline and evaluation document to be discussed in Chapter 5.

Figure 3.2 Common Operational Areas and Metrics Improved Through S&OP

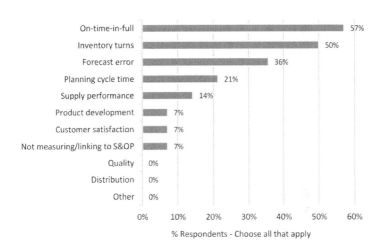

% Respondents - Choose all that apply

Source: Nexview Consulting Survey, 2014

Magnitude of benefits

The magnitude of improvements naturally depends upon where your current baseline is, but for concentrated efforts, I normally see improvements in the 5 – 25% range that can be fully realized over a period of 6-12 months. You should start seeing some progression on results much earlier though, perhaps in 1-3 months with the Hawthorne effect contributing at some level.

Figure 3.3 Common Financial Areas and Metrics Improved Through S&OP

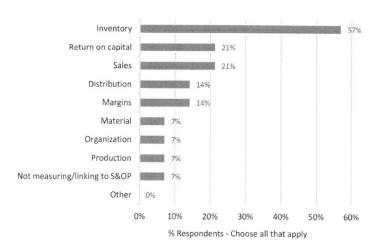

Source: Nexview Consulting Survey, 2014

I'll discuss some techniques for determining magnitudes in the assessment section below. Here's some data from a recent survey that surveyed respondents' perceptions on the size of potential supply chain improvement benefits.

Figure 3.4 Magnitude of Results from S&OP

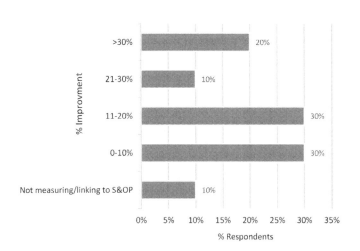

Source: Nexview Consulting Survey, 2014

Conducting an assessment

You may very well have a set of underperforming KPIs or be in repeated "fire-fighting" mode that may be the impetus to launch an improvement effort. Before launching into an improvement project, conducting an assessment is very important to align your group around the current state, what the gaps are, and what filling those gaps would be worth. It's a critical part of the change process and if you're inclined to seek outside help, many consulting firms will insist on it if quantified benefits are to be part of the dance.

I'll give you an overview of the key steps and components, but the details of conducting an assessment including details on specific studies are beyond the intended scope of this book.

Suffice to say that the assessment is the basis for your improvement initiative. Without it, your project is at risk for discord among team members, scope creep, and perhaps even being cancelled when the next priority in the business arises that needs resources.

If you skip the assessment up-front, you'll do a fragmented assessment anyway within the project as you'll need analysis to back up your assertions for change management purposes. You won't always see this coming and you'll be in reactive mode here when you hit a question or challenge from someone in a position to do so. You may as well budget and resource it. Do it right, and do it at the beginning. The typical flow of an assessment is shown below.

Techniques for determining magnitudes of improvement opportunities

After you've developed some hypotheses from interviews, completed a best practice assessment, conducted process analysis, etc., it's time to zero in on what you believe to be the highest impact areas and attach some numbers to them. There is some uncertainty and experience needed here, but by using a combination of techniques listed below, you can usually get to something credible. Some of the techniques that are used in completing assessments are described in the next few paragraphs.

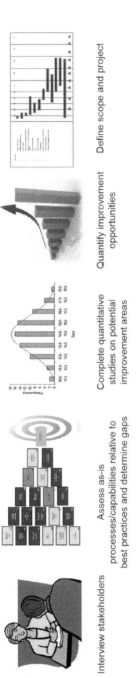

Figure 3.5 Key Steps in an Assessment

Examining historical trends

Showing historical trends and determining what would need to happen to get back to a previously demonstrated higher performing state. This is largely an estimation.

Using benchmarks

It's easy to want to gravitate to benchmarks and get the comfort of being able to point to data that's allegedly credible. It's easy to say "if they can do it, so can we." While there is some truth to this, you also need to be careful about comparing their apples to your oranges.

Definitions may be different and the business situations may be different. I'd also be careful of claims that some may make of "our proprietary database based on our vast experience." That vast experience may have come from some consulting manager's credibility play in response to a client request, which triggered an edict to a junior consultant who did a Google search the night before.

Internal benchmarks may be better. It's okay to look at business units in your company and look at what they're doing. Benchmarks are data points, they aren't the Holy Grail. Look at them in the context of the other items, and make a judgment based on all the inputs.

Building models

This is a little better if you can put something on a spreadsheet and make a calculation. The best models are those that can be validated by using inputs at the current level of performance to give the outputs that duplicate the current measured state.

Inventory can be modeled for example. The inputs (e.g. demand, demand and supply variability, lead times, and service levels) can tweaked in your model to determine what inventories could be with the corresponding improvements in the inputs.

Distribution might be another one to model if you're wasting money on non-nearest shipments, internal transfers between warehouses, or perhaps not using optimized routes or preferred carriers. Determine the excess cost of all that silliness and estimate a fraction that can be saved if you do X, Y, and Z. Sometimes sufficient time isn't budgeted to build the models that we'd like, and less certain methods must be used.

Examining an audit sample

You may not have time to look at every situation, so you do a detailed analysis on a sample set and assume the same conditions exist in the entire set. You then calculate the benefit on the audit sample and just scale it.

Conducting observations

I'm talking about in-person observations here. Data observations would be classified as a form of audit as described above. In supply chain assessments, observations are used to understand issues more deeply and for organizational improvement opportunities. Opportunities range from process improvement to clarifying and realigning roles and responsibilities, to headcount evaluation.

Figure 3.6 shows a sample benefits summary chart of some areas throughout the supply chain and ultimately linked through S&OP. There are some terms in the chart that we'll discuss in more detail in the subsequent chapters. It's important to present a benefit summary in a simple, but comprehensive manner and this is a format that I've found works well. When I give talks on results subjects, the cameras normally come out when I show this slide.

Putting your benefits on a timeline

Now that we have the benefit areas and the associated improvement targets, it's time to determine how long it will take to achieve them. Obviously the other variable here is resources. Scope, resources, and timing are inherently related. Like good, fast, and cheap, you can pick your favorite two. Our benefit areas should give us the scope, so develop a project plan, estimate resources, and put the achievement of your benefits on a timeline.

A detailed discussion on developing the project plan isn't the intent of this book, and every one of them is different. For complex supply chain change programs in large organizations (multiple business units and perhaps > $500MM in sales), you should be thinking about assessment periods ranging from 6 to 16 weeks and implementation periods ranging from 40 to 60 weeks.

To establish monthly "plan" values for annually recurring benefits, I'll normally estimate a percent of total plan that is

Benefit Area	Baseline ($MM)	Impactable ($MM)	Operational Levers	% Savings	P&L ($MM)	One Time Cash Flow ($MM)
Increased Sales	3,250	N/A	▪Improved management of promotions ▪Reduce stock-outs ▪Improved OTIF ▪Reduce lead times ▪Customer segmentation & service policies	0.5 – 1%	1.9 – 3.9 @ 12% margin	
Procurement - Direct Material	1,479	1,109	▪Alliance management ▪RFPs ▪Consolidate suppliers spend across sites	3 – 5%	33.3 – 55.5	
Procurement - Indirect	38.0	38.0	▪Leveraged spend across sites ▪RFQs/RFPs	3 – 5%	1.1 – 1.9	
Distribution & Logistics	96.8	72.5	▪Network optimization, reduce stock points ▪3PL sourcing, preferred carrier management	4 – 7%	2.9 – 5.1	
Organization - Direct and Indirect	667.9	333.9	▪Reorganization ▪Centralized supply chain organization	5 – 10%	16.7 – 33.4	
Inventory – Finished Goods	227.5	204.8	▪Min/Max settings and reorders points ▪Improve forecasting ▪Improve DRP	10 – 20%	2.1 – 4.1 @ 10% WACC	20.5 – 40.9
Inventory – WIP and Raw Material	97.5	92.6	▪Min/Max settings and reorder points ▪Increase VMI and consignment ▪Improve production scheduling ▪Reduce supplier lead times	5 – 10%	0.5 – 0.9 @ 10% WACC	4.6 – 9.3
Total P&L Cost Base, *Benefit*	**2,282**	**1,553**		**4 – 7%**	**58.5 – 104.8**	
One Time Cash Base, *Benefit*	**422.5**	**390.0**		**6 - 13%**		**25.1 – 50.2**

Figure 3.6 Sample Benefits Summary Chart

linked to the achievement of project milestones. From the monthly annualized values, you can calculate what that would require each month on a cumulative basis.

We'll talk more about cumulative and annualized benefits in the next chapter, so don't worry if this isn't crystal clear right now. Just know that to get a payback curve, you need to know the total benefits you are getting and costs you are incurring each month. If your initial resource estimates turn out to be wrong (i.e. not available), you just need to iterate your scope (project plan) and benefits timeline such that all three are in balance to the best of your estimation.

With your quantified benefits case set against a timeline you are creating the necessary justification for resources and action. This is your business case for change and you're now in a position to calculate the other parameters that executive decision makers like to know such as breakeven point, IRR, and/or NPV.

Large investments in change including internal and potentially external resources to make major improvements in your company won't happen without these numbers. Just as project costs need to be budgeted perhaps for the next period, benefits should also go into the next budget cycle.

If benefits become part of the next budget, leaders will be committed to them. Plus, committing benefits to a timeline creates the necessary sense of urgency to achieve them during the specified period. These are good things.

Furthermore, when you get into the project, benefits on a timeline also give you the needed foundation for discussion when other "options" your project resources arise. You may be structuring your results driven S&OP and supply chain improvement project in combination with an IT project.

If the IT project (beware of the ubiquitous SAP upgrade that is frequently in play!) or something else starts to take your resources, you can have an executive level discussion about how the benefits curve will shift out. This input will help them prioritize the best course of action for the business.

Here's a sample straight payback curve that simply nets the timing of the inbound and outbound cash flows. I use the term "straight payback" to mean that I haven't discounted cash flows within the project horizon (typically less than 1 year), but when I talk about a multi-year NPV, I have applied a discount rate to the net recurring annualized benefit similar to any other NPV analysis. You can check with your finance person on how you'd like to do this and the appropriate discount rate for your application.

Organizational dynamics during an assessment

Pointing out benefit areas and quantifying numbers associated with gaps is great in the spirit of generating more results and improving the business. It also has another side. It can also say to the manager in that area something like "Gee, we just came in and found all this opportunity in your area, have you been asleep?"

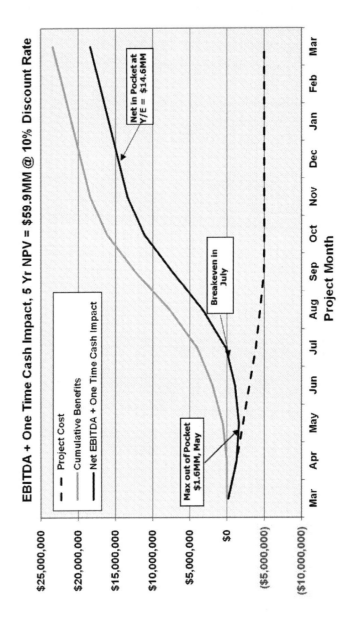

Figure 3.7 Sample Payback Curve for a Change Program

A large company CEO I came to respect very much once said to me, "I'm paying my staff, aren't they supposed to do these things?" This question begs the one about why the field of management consulting exists so I won't go there, but how do you think most people react to these great opportunities for the company that have gone unrealized under their watch?

They often become defensive and don't think that they exist. People love to point out gaps in other areas, but no one likes having their baby called ugly. Data backed-up by some modeling helps here, but you still get into it with them.

Benefit magnitudes, timelines for achieving them, and resources required make for some spirited conversations. Sometimes the conversations never happen because a junior person can't have it with a senior person, or rationality gives way to politics. Sometimes consultants are brought in exclusively for this purpose.

It's okay to either shoot the consulting messenger or point to their wisdom depending upon where you sit. Consulting teams aren't always in agreement amongst themselves either. Consulting firms have their dynamics too, and don't think for a second that consultants just move on to the next client without repercussions if something doesn't work out. We're on the line too. Perhaps more stories for another day, but you get the idea. Leaders know all this and realize it's a process to be worked through given all the agendas in play. It's not perfect, but the outcome is generally better than doing nothing.

In an assessment you simply won't have time to get everyone on board with everything, but you need enough to move forward. The larger changes and organizational alignment is a process that takes months in large organizations. Better build that into your project plan.

You can see from the discussion above that identifying benefit areas, quantifying them, and putting an improvement effort around them is both an art and a science. I guess it's one reason why the field of operations improvement management consulting exists. If you're feeling a little queasy about committing to the numbers and the timeline of the benefits curve, you're not alone, but it's what leaders do all the time.

Coming from an engineering background, where mistakes could not only lose money, but could also result in explosions in the wrong places, I struggled early in my consulting career with the uncertainty around benefits cases. Leaders in business manage uncertainty and risk every day.

It's their job and the ones who are successful get to stay, perhaps advance, the others don't. You just need to decide if you want to have some faith, play this game or not, and set your goals accordingly.

I suggest having some faith in your assumptions and capabilities, and go for it with the best information possible. With that, we'll need some techniques for measuring and managing the results as the improvements are made. This will hopefully postpone the graying of your hair and will be needed to help you with some of those organizational dynamics we talked about.

Takeaways from Chapter 3 – Identifying and Quantifying Your Results Case

- Results from S&OP are accelerated and more traceable when S&OP efforts are combined with improvements the underlying processes.
- Link the process improvements to operating metrics, and link the operating metrics to the financial ones.
- Use S&OP as the platform to keep visibility on results, integrate efforts, and align focus where needed
- An assessment is a methodical process that will align and ground the improvement effort around a defined scope with a defined benefits case.
- A variety of methods should be used as inputs to improvement targets.
- Improvement targets need to be put on a timeline for a corresponding defined scope and level of resourcing.
- Once the benefits are put on a timeline, you can present an executive picture to evaluate a project return.
- Benefits cases can get emotional among varying agendas, and while insights and experience are good, the strongest cases are made when the data does the talking.

FOUR

The Key Components of Results Tracking

The next couple of chapters get into some detail on results tracking. The concepts apply to any improvement program, not just S&OP, but I'll reemphasize the point about connecting results to the process. Going back to our body analogy, these techniques are food to make the S&OP mind sharper and the skeleton stronger. No food and the body dies.

Results tracking is no easy task and requires work to set-up and maintain. It may seem cut and dry, just count and record quantities, but in complex supply chain interactions under changing business conditions, it can also be an art depending upon your business situation and your philosophical approach. Let's start with the fundamental building blocks and discuss the terminology.

Components of results

The following terminology describes the components of results tracking and should be included in your vernacular. This terminology will be integral to the tracking tools I'll discuss in the next chapter.

Baseline

The baseline is the datum from which to measure improvement. It is often a historical average or cumulative value over a defined period. When determining a baseline, the first step is to look at a time series plot of historical data. Certainly throw out any outlier points, and pick a representative period to look at. For income statement benefits, this could be the ending value from last year or last twelve months, or maybe an average of the last couple years.

For balance sheet accounts (e.g. inventory), it could be the current value or perhaps an average of the last 12 month ending balances. You want to be careful about showing an excessive positive or negative benefit at the start of the project though, so compare your average to the current value.

Sometimes during a longer assessment, because of a heightened awareness (especially if consultants are running around), improvements resulting in measurable improvements can magically appear (recall that Hawthorne thing). In these cases, you may want to set the time to start counting benefits back to the beginning of the assessment.

Beware of the budget

Sometimes company leaders want to use the current budget as the baseline. Their logic being that the current mode of operation is already going to deliver the current budget, so any improvement effort should deliver something beyond that. This can be a little like looking at a wasp's nest building on the roof eve above you, but not doing anything about it (I have one overhead as I write this). It may not sting you today, but the future is a different story.

Let's face it, budgeting processes aren't always efficient in companies. Hopes, dreams, management edict, and who knows what else can be in there. It's best to use actual historical data. A couple times I've been backed into the budget baseline corner and it usually means more time on explanations later as you deal with project complexities and on top of that, likely a need to revisit all the faults that went into the budget.

If this happens to you and you have the luxury of being able to change the benefits case, you should reduce it by the amount that a data-based historical baseline and the current budget differ. I'm assuming of course that the budget is more aggressive than the historical data here, has anyone ever seen it the other way?

You can start to see how some judgment is going to factor in to this thing I call results tracking, and I'm just getting warmed up.

Target

This is your value of the benefit quantity to be achieved at some future period, usually at the end of an improvement project.

Plan

This is a progression over time of the planned value of the benefit and how it moves from the baseline to the target. The plan is the plan, and it doesn't change once you set it. It's like a budget in that sense and is the yardstick by which success is measured.

Forecast

A business plan or budget is great when you release it at the beginning of the year and then as the year progresses, "stuff" happens. Results-based projects are no different. Consider the forecast to be the most current estimate of where the benefits will end up. When something in the project or business changes (and it will), executives need to know, where the effort is really going to end up.

Actuals

This is the actual value of the benefit quantity measured. Seems straight forward enough, but there are a couple different approaches depending upon your philosophy towards benefit recognition. I'll explain shortly.

I'll use this terminology as represented above in this book, but I'll also say don't get too hung up on terminology if you need to adjust it to fit the terminology of your culture. For example, in some cultures "plan" means the business budget and using "plan" to refer to a project benefit commitment is too confusing. Just use something else for the project thing (e.g. commitment or other synonym). The main this is that you have the components above and everyone is clear on what they refer to.

Applications to KPI management

Note that your KPI scorecard should have the same components, except maybe for forecast. Let me explain. I just mentioned that "plan" often has a budget connotation. As we know, budgets don't change once they're set (perhaps in rare circumstances), so if you have a KPI that's also a budgeted quantity, you should fix "plan" and use "forecast" for your latest projection.

Many operational KPIs are not budgeted quantities, in which case "plan" and "target" can change as you need to change them. In this case, "plan" is just a time-phased incremental path on how your KPI will be achieved going from a baseline value to the target value. Again, the concepts are important, but the terminology really isn't, use the nomenclature that best fits your culture.

Recurring and one-time benefits

Recurring benefits are related to the income statement (e.g. transportation savings), whereas one-time results are usually related to the balance sheet (e.g. inventory reduction, reduction in days-of-sale outstanding). It's also possible to have a one-time benefit to the income statement in some situations (e.g. perhaps you caught up on outstanding warranty claims, or got a one-time rebate or deal on something).

Cumulative and annualized benefits

When we talk about recurring benefits, we also express them as being cumulative or annualized. *Cumulative* benefits are the sum total of benefits to date. Here's a simple example.

Table 4.1 Cumulative Benefit Example		
Month	Benefit This Month	Cumulative Benefit
1	3	3
2	5	8
3	10	18

Note how the benefit increment increases each month. This indicates that improvements are accelerating. At some point when all improvements have been implemented, the monthly benefit will level off and stay constant from month to month. We call that hitting "run rate".

For every month whether in the ramp-up or steady-state period, there is also an *annualized benefit*. This is the benefit that would occur at that point in time on an annualized basis if no further improvements were made. In the table below there's a simple example of taking this month's benefit and multiplying by 12 to represent the annualized benefit at that point in time.

Table 4.2 Cumulative and Annualized Benefit Example			
Month	Benefit This Month	Cumulative Benefit	Annualized Benefit
1	3	3	36
2	5	8	60
3	10	18	120
4	12	30	144

Table 4.2 Cumulative and Annualized Benefit Example			
5	15	45	180
6	15	60	180
7	15	75	180

From the data above, you can see that the benefits for the effort were fully realized in month 5 and will continue to accrue at a constant run rate of 15/month, or 180/year in perpetuity. In this example, I've kept it simple for illustrative purposes, but sometime you may want to use a rolling average of monthly benefits. See later discussion when this can be helpful.

Philosophy on recognizing results

There are two different philosophical approaches to benefit recognition that apply to improvement programs as follows.

Philosophy 1 - Link benefits directly to process or project activities

With this approach, you want to measure results that came directly from activities related to S&OP and/or an improvement project. It can become complicated because your project does not happen in a vacuum. Business moves on as you're making improvements and business conditions change.

Changing business conditions

On large complex supply chain projects of any duration (say greater than 6 months). Something will change relative to your baseline condition. Here are a few examples:

Fuel prices change – Wow, transportation benefits look great if prices went down, not so good if prices go up.

Commodity price swings – Same thing as fuel costs. Say suppliers want to impose a 5% price hike, but a great procurement effort holds them to 3%. Is this a 2% benefit, or a negative 3% benefit over the baseline? Hmmm..., I'll bet you'll get a few different opinions here. I'll vote for a 2% cost avoidance.

Sales skyrocketed – Great for the business, but more inventory was needed to support those sales, so it went up. Measure inventory turns right? Base the benefit on that? Yes, you can non-dimensionalize operating metrics, but you'll still have to explain something when we translate that to money.

Sales tanked – If there are no sales, then inventory doesn't get worked down, is that the fault of the improvement project? (Maybe - if this wasn't forecasted, but you get the idea.)

There was a corporate M&A or divestiture event, the asset and cost bases changed, should you change your baselines? Probably.

You're starting to get the picture. Results management is often not so easy. Even if a core team has a real good handle on all these things, what are the chances that key stakeholders and executives who aren't as close to this will? You will explain this every time you get significantly behind or above plan, and explaining all this to them takes time and can sometimes get hairy.

Table 4.3 Factors External to the Project That Can Influence Results		
Benefit Area	**Benefit Metrics**	**Potential Outside Influence**
Sales	■ Revenue growth ■ Reduction in lost sales ■ On-time-in-full	■ Market price changes ■ Macro-economic effects ■ Market demand ■ Internal integrating gaps in performance (e.g. sales effectiveness or production performance)
Inventory	■ Inventory turns ■ Days on hand ■ Obsolete inventory ■ Stock-outs	■ Market effects as described above ■ Changes in COGS ■ Production sourcing or distribution decisions
Distribution & Logistics	■ Unit transportation costs ■ Warehouse costs	■ Fuel price changes ■ Volume changes
Procurement	■ Spend ■ Item costs ■ Supplier lead times ■ Supplier OTIF	■ Market changes influencing price ■ Supplier performance
Production (S&OP Related)	■ Throughput/ cycle time ■ Unit costs ■ Plan adherence ■ Plan attainment ■ Overtime	■ Organizational downsizing ■ Union issues ■ Demand changes ■ Production sourcing changes

Negative benefits

The situation gets even worse when a benefit category goes negative. It happens more than you might think at first. Think about this for a minute, what could a negative benefit possibly mean? I've had many discussions with client executives and controllers on this point. If you think about it, it necessarily means one of the following:

1. What you are doing on the project is HURTING THE BUSINESS, thus creating a negative benefit. You should stop doing S&OP and any improvement activities. That seems silly.

2. Your baseline or actual measurement is wrong, perhaps something changed in the business, or your baseline was just not representative of the true initial condition.

If this happens, you should re-evaluate the baseline or actual measurement in light of current business conditions. I'm not saying it's okay to change baselines willy-nilly, but sometimes it's warranted. The other thing you can do is adjust recorded actuals with "factors" that represent adjustments to account for changes that have occurred relative to the baseline. I recommend one-off baseline changes rather than repeated application and explanation of "doctoring" actuals.

You can also say, there really is no benefit here and just zero it out from the benefit case, rather than record negative benefits and penalize the project each month. Of course this means something else has to over-deliver to make the overall target.

Rolling averages

For annualized benefits, sometimes it's a good idea to use a rolling average of the monthly actuals when computing the annualized value. I advise this if the values are up and down from month to month. You want to show values that accurately represent the trend in annualized savings, not some up and down thing that looks wonky.

On the balance sheet side, inventory is a good example where I have used rolling averages since it can go up and down from month to month. I've often used 2 or 3 month rolling averages to represent and actual benefit state.

Rolling averages have the effect of dampening variability, while showing trend. I advise against using periods longer than 2 or 3 months though because you carry historical values just too long, and it can take too long to show the actual progress relative to the project timeline.

<u>Pros and cons of Philosophy 1</u>

The benefit of Philosophy 1 is that you are linking activities to benefits as closely as you can and are adjusting for conditions that are out of the control of the project team. The downside is that a lot of work can go into this depending on what happens.

The other downside is that you can show good results for the project, but they don't show up in the financials. Nothing annoys a management team more than a wildly successful project and an underperforming business. If you go with Philosophy 1, you still need to keep your eye on the financials and be aware of any deviations.

Philosophy 2 - Take straight measurements of actuals

From a measurement standpoint, this approach is much easier. To measure financial benefits, you simply take the numbers at face value. Typically, these are values from general ledger accounts and you can just turn the task over to accounting. You still have to have good initial baselines, but most or all of the adjustment discussion above doesn't apply.

Obviously simplicity is the advantage here, but when actuals are above plan, people say – "Yeah, but the project didn't cause that, that was caused by the price increase/market/event/pick your reason, blah, blah, blah." When results are below plan, those invested in the project say the opposite. Usually, their points start with "It's not our fault blah, blah, blah."

In addition to being easy, another benefit of this approach is that, G/L balances are typically how executives are judged. Too bad if the economy tanked or the weather was bad. The mindset here needs to be that we don't really care where the success comes from, we're just going to do everything we can and if we hit targets we're happy, and if we don't, then we just lose. End of story.

Agree on your philosophical approach

Whichever way you decide to proceed, you need to have frank discussions about the approaches and their implications. Create a chart like the one in Table 4.4, and get concurrence from the sponsor and other executive stakeholders. We'll talk about sign-off in Chapter 5.

Table 4.4 Considerations for Tracking Philosophy	
Adjust for factors external to the project	■ A lot of work ■ Complicated to explain ■ Rigorous on-going attention ■ Closest link between project activities and results ■ Risk losing financial traceability to the G/L
Adjust for factors external to the project	■ Easier ■ People will have all sorts of on-going opinions as to the positive or negative impacts of external factors ■ What investors will look at and what management really lives with

CASE STUDY – CHANGING CONDITIONS AND BASELINES

I had the chance to lead a large, multi-site productivity improvement project in the mining industry. It wasn't supply chain, but it is a good example of how baselines, targets, and results tracking can go. While our project had several objectives, the results case was primarily based on improving output per labor hour and output per machine hour. Seems straight forward enough. We did our best to baseline the productivity under the current ways of working, made our process and management system improvements, and measured productivity rates again to determine the benefit.

All of a sudden, we would hit an unplanned change in terrain, maybe rock where we were expecting dirt. Hmmm...., it takes longer to dig through rock. Maybe it rained excessively on a particular job and we didn't baseline productivity working in the rain and mud during Week 1. On later projects, we had the blueprint for the new ways of working and put it in place right at the beginning. Since this was a new project, there wasn't any history of working "the old way".

Projects were all slightly different and we couldn't always use baseline productivity data from prior projects. How do you baseline in this case? We certainly weren't going to start working the old inefficient way for the purpose of establishing a baseline.

Front line managers and supervisors initially balked at our measurement efforts, but their upper management clarified priorities and we won them over, making them more successful in the process. The client had made promises to investors based on our results case, and my employer had put significant consulting fees at risk based on the results case. There was a lot of pressure all around to get this right.

We made our best assumptions when we had to and changed our baselines when we had to. It wasn't always completely black and white. In addition to the normal huge workload of a major change program often working in remote locations, the results tracking part was a large time investment for all involved on both the consulting and client sides. The project ended up being very successful. The extra effort to count the dollars was completely worth it.

Takeaways from Chapter 4 – The Key Components of Results

- Each result area needs to have a baseline, target, plan, and forecast.
- Results are expressed in cumulative and annualized terms.

- There are many things outside of the control of the project team that can influence supply chain results.
- Adjustments for outside influences can be time consuming and difficult to adjust for, while taking values straight from the G/L doesn't always link project activities to results. You need to pick your poison.
- A solid tracking tool with documentation of benefit components and assumptions will be needed to keep track of all of this.

FIVE

Your Results Tracking Toolkit

By now you are beginning to see a little about what we're up against to keep some order in all of this. Next I'll talk about some important tools/templates that are essential for documenting, organizing, and reporting your benefits.

Baseline & evaluation documents

Agreement as discussed on baselines and benefit calculation methodologies is not enough. When something changes two or three months after a verbal agreement, the recollections of those involved will generally not be consistent. Baselines and evaluation methods need to be documented and signed by the executive who owns delivery of that benefit, accounting who'll track it, and the person who came up with the numbers and methodology (maybe a project manager or area lead).

Without signatures the originator of the document owns it and that person is too low in the organization. With the right signatures, the right person owns it and anyone else who needs to agree (e.g. accounting) will agree now and later when it matters.

Table 5.1 Contents of Baseline & Evaluation Documents	
BASELINE SECTION	**BASELINE EVALUATION SECTION**
1. Baseline period	1. Calculation method
2. Scope	2. Period that tracking begins
3. Method for computing	3. Methods for adjustment/normalization
4. Any normalization, adjustments, or data excluded	4. Data source
5. Source of the data	5. Frequency of reporting
6. Baseline value or amount	6. Key operating levers and metrics
7. Assumptions	7. Executive accountable for the result
	8. Person tracking the benefit
	9. Assumptions

Results should be kept in a centrally managed tool

I'm talking about a custom spreadsheet here. These can get somewhat elaborate depending upon how may workstreams and results areas there are. They need to contain baselines, targets, plans, forecasts and actuals, benefit summaries, cumulative, annual, and one-time values. All of this data should be shown in monthly buckets that flow to graphical and summary charts for easy executive presentation.

To create the tracking tool, it's best to enlist the support of the person(s) who will be tracking results on a regular basis. Perhaps a project manager gives the tool builder a sample template containing one benefit area and asks them to build out the others and link sheets, sum benefit areas up etc. A team member from finance who's good at Excel and financial modeling is a great choice.

One benefit number

Recall when we created the benefits summary table from the assessment, we specified ranges for the benefits. When we're at the tool creation stage, we really need to pick a number from that range. You don't want to have "low" and "high" plan and forecast curves and triple the size of your results tracking tool. You can keep the high end of the range as a stretch target and keep it visible as desired, but I recommend committing to one number and putting that profile in the tracker.

To arrive at a single number within a range ask yourself, how solid was this part of the assessment? Was something modeled or more estimated? How much resistance was there around the benefit area? How much do you need to make the benefits case compelling? How much will the executive leader in that area sign-up for? These all factor into your one number decision.

Once the tool is created, you'll have to develop a process for who will update it and what that schedule is. Hold an appropriate training session and follow-up as needed. The schedule may be slightly different by benefit area depending upon when data become available. On larger projects with many benefit areas, the tracker is normally first populated by the lead of each area and then transitioned to accounting.

It's important that area leads remain engaged in the benefits associated with the activities they are leading. The downside of this is the more people that are involved, the more people you will chase each month to have your results tracking tool updated on time.

You can set up an informal report-out meeting to have area leads talk to their respective areas. This is to ensure understanding and compliance, I'll discuss how to handle executive reporting in Chapter 6.

There are usually detailed schedules for each benefit area behind the summary sheet that add up various components too. Area leads and finance need to be in these too. Put some access control on your tools and make back-up copies. When lots of hands are moving across a crowded picnic table, someone usually knocks over a glass.

Figure 5.1 is a summary sheet across several benefit areas. Behind each benefit area there should be a sheet in the Excel workbook (or somewhere) that tallies up the value from however many components are involved. When recording actuals the annualized values are calculated from the cumulative values by the means you've decided (recall discussion in last chapter). You can then total it up and plot it as you'd like.

From your detailed tracking spreadsheet, you'll need to create a summary for executive presentation. If you show the details of a tracking tool as pictured above to an executive or the uninitiated, their eyes will just glaze over and they'll rate you low on your ability to present executive information.

Normally I show a summary table such as that shown below for the current month, and a graph that shows a plot of the total over the course of the project (see Figures 5.2 and 5.3). You might also want to show plots of specific areas that are behind to get the needed attention and action. Just make sure it's not too detailed.

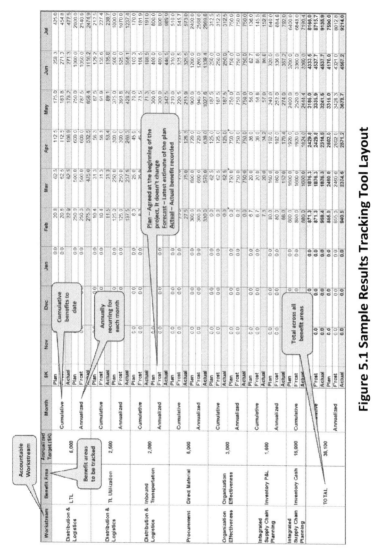

Figure 5.1 Sample Results Tracking Tool Layout

See the note in the Introduction for a link to download this spreadsheet.

Summary scorecard

From your detailed tracking spreadsheet, you'll need to create a summary for executive presentation. If you show the details of a tracking tool as pictured above to an executive or the uninitiated, their eyes will just glaze over and they'll rate you low on your ability to present executive information.

Normally I show a summary table such as that shown below for the current month, and a graph that shows a plot of the total over the course of the project (see Figures 5.2 and 5.3). You might also want to show plots of specific areas that are behind to get the needed attention and action. Just make sure it's not too detailed.

Here are a couple of examples. In Table 5.2, we see Project "S&OP Align". The project is fortunate to be ahead of plan at this point and the forecast looks good. The forecast Y/E values are actually above the originally planned Y/E values (not shown). The chart just gets too busy if you have too many columns. You can voiceover the point about being above plan and show the total for all benefit areas on the graph.

Table 5.2 Project "S&OP Align" Benefits - July						
Benefit Area	**Cumulative ($000s)**			**Annually Recurring ($000s)**		
	Plan	Actual	Y/E Forecast	Plan	Actual	Y/E Forecast
Distribution & Logistics - LTL	425	477	2,347	2,000	2,475	5,500
Distribution & Logistics – TL Utilization	213	239	1,173	1,000	1,237	2,500

Table 5.2 Project "S&OP Align" Benefits - July					
Distribution & Logistics – Inbound Trans	170	191	939	800	990	2,200
Procurement – Direct Material	510	573	2,816	2,400	2,970	6,600
Organization Effectiveness	313	313	1,375	750	750	3,000
Inventory - P&L	136	153	751	640	792	1,760
Inventory - Cash	6,400	7,190	17,600	n/a	n/a	n/a
TOTAL Recurring	1,767	1,946	9,401	7590	9214	21,560
TOTAL One-Time	6,400	7,290	17,600	n/a	n/a	n/a

Cumulative benefits

Let's take a look at the benefit curves for a moment. First consider the cumulative curve. You can see that we have a project that started in November and then started to recognize benefits in February of the following year. Perhaps the project started out small through the holiday period with a core team and then ramped up in the New Year.

In the first two months, the core team may have been getting the benefits tracking system in place and getting leaders on-board with it. Leaders may have been allocating resources to the project and the holidays were also in the way. This isn't the ideal way to start a project (big bang is better), but this can happen.

Plus, it takes a couple months to begin generating some "quick wins". Benefits typically have a lower slope in the

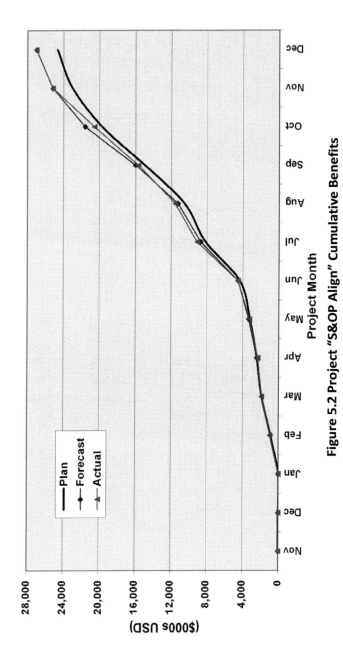

Figure 5.2 Project "S&OP Align" Cumulative Benefits

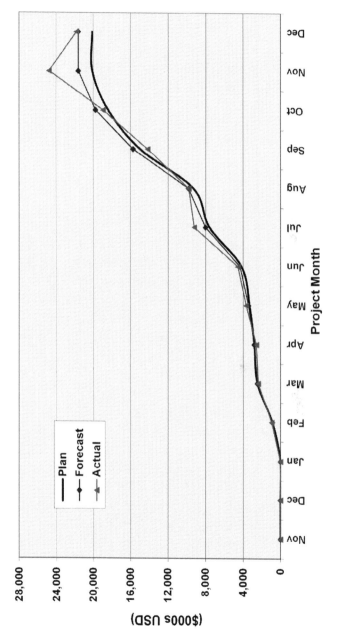

Figure 5.3 Project "S&OP Align" Annualized Benefits

earlier months and then accelerate once the project gains momentum. As the project benefits reach full run rate (recall this is when the monthly increment is constant), you'll see a constant slope and amount each month. In this model, this only occurs at the end (December). Note also that the one-time inventory benefits are in this curve, which is why the cumulative curve exceeds the annualized amounts. You won't see this in Year 2 after the inventory benefit has been fully realized.

Annualized benefits

The annualized curve is a little more volatile. In this model, I didn't use rolling averages and that shows most right at the end. The plan was to reach steady-state or run rate in November. See how the plan and forecast curves level off. A little dose of reality set-in and the project was over plan in November and under plan in December. This tells us that we're not quite at steady state yet and you'll have to dissect this little nugget before going into that steering team meeting.

You'll certainly get a question about the drop-off. You also are likely to get questions if your planned curves aren't smooth. "Why isn't the curve smooth, what are those bumps?" You could draw your plans to be some straight linear or nice looking exponential curve fit, but remember, we are trying to match benefit quantities with project activities and milestones.

Doing this and providing this explanation when asked demonstrates the thought that went into the estimate. Maybe the curve gapped up in one month because organizational benefits were recognized (layoffs), or a large procurement benefit kicked-in. Just remind people of things like this. In this case, the important thing to remind people of, is that it looks like the project exceeded target, so bonuses for the project team!

A project that's behind schedule

Here's another example of a different project (hypothetical of course), "S&OP Perform". Note that in spite of its name, is it underperforming in a few areas. This is the more common case. Some areas will underperform, while others will hopefully over-deliver. The most important thing to a steering team is that the project total is at or above plan.

Note that yellow and red exceptions are highlighted based on tolerances you set and communicate. After some quick recognition of what is ahead of plan, you want to have discussion on exception items to ensure they get back on track. Projects are a lot more fun to work on when they're at or ahead of plan.

Just a little more on the inventory benefit. Recall that an inventory reduction is a one-time balance sheet (or cash) reduction, but the inventory carrying cost is an income statement benefit and would recur as long as inventory reductions are sustained. The recurring benefit is a future carrying cost avoidance. In this example, I've just used 10% as a carrying cost, but we know inventory carrying costs are generally higher. The literature talks about inventory carrying costs in the 20-25% range when you add in things like asset base taxes, insurance, warehousing, and shrinkage.

If you are in a business unit of a larger corporation, you likely have a corporate allocation charge for your inventory.

Table 5.3 Project "S&OP Perform" Benefits - July						
Benefit Area	Cumulative ($MM)			Annually Recurring ($MM)		
	Plan	Actual	Y/E Forecast	Plan	Actual	Y/E Forecast
Sales	1.2	1.3	5.7	2.0	2.4	2.6
Inventory (Cash)	4.2	3.5	6.2	n/a	n/a	n/a
Inventory (Recurring Financing)	0.4	0.35	0.6	1.2	1.0	1.2
Distribution & Logistics	2.2	2.0	3.7	3.1	3.0	5.0
Procurement	6.0	6.7	8.2	9.2	10.6	12.5
TOTAL Recurring	9.8	10.4	18.2	15.5	17.0	21.3
TOTAL One-Time	4.2	3.5	6.2	n/a	n/a	n/a

If this is the case, use that rate. The specific percentage to use is a discussion and agreement with finance.

If you don't have a specific percent charge for this in place already, you may want to run a tally on this yourself if you can, as finance can be conservative on this value. This can be a lot of work and get into some cost accounting too. Relative to the other benefit areas, the carrying cost benefit usually isn't too much. I normally just get a verbal agreement and move on to next 1000 things on the list.

Table 5.4 Recap of Results Tracking Tools	
Project Benefit Summary	▪ Succinctly summarizes benefits from an assessment ▪ Shows preliminary baselines, available spend to impact, key operational levers to achieve benefits, and often a range for each benefit category ▪ May also be used later in the project to remind people of commitments if necessary
Project Payback Curve	▪ Shows the sum of project cash flows over the course of the project ▪ Used to justify the investment in the project and ROI
Baseline & Evaluation Methodology Document	▪ Documents how baselines were arrived at, how benefits are to be tracked, and any assumptions ▪ Signed off by accountable executive, project manager/area lead who's responsible, and finance for tracking
Results Tracking Tool	▪ Spreadsheet of record for tracking benefit parameters over time ▪ Combination of detail with a summary sheet ▪ Limit access to those populating actuals and managing results
Summary Chart	▪ One page summary for executive briefings and reports ▪ Highlights exceptions ▪ Supported by a graph that shows summary benefits over the course of the project
KPI Scorecard	▪ Used more for on-going management of the business ▪ Has a baseline, target, plan, and actual (could add forecast if the KPI is a budgeted item and you need to retain original plan)

Table 5.4 Recap of Results Tracking Tools
■ Needs to be documented similar to project benefits ■ Numerical report supported by graphs ■ Highlights exceptions ■ Shows some history and the future plan

Frequency of tracking for project benefits

The goal is to find the balance among having enough information to track progress and enable intermediate course correction, the usefulness of the information, and the work that's required to track it. Monthly tracking for supply chain financial benefits is normally the best balance. Operating metrics can often be looked at more frequently (e.g. on-time-in-full). Sometimes spend in certain areas (e.g. procurement and transportation) is can also easy to get in an automated fashion.

The interval for reviewing operating metrics should correspond to the interval that your actions can influence them. For example you may not be able to influence inventory daily if your production schedule is frozen on a weekly basis, but you may be able to measure production schedule adherence on a daily basis to take intermediate action to influence the weekly inventory KPI.

Intermediate data points give an indication of trend to enable action during the month, but if you're using adjustments or need to make other interpretations as discussed in Chapter 4, you'll start spending a lot of time here. Try to look for indicators throughout the month to enable course corrections, but I don't recommend anything more than monthly for the "official" numbers.

Applications to KPI management

Many of the principles discussed in this chapter also apply to KPI management. KPIs would have similar baseline and evaluation documents. There's less of an emphasis on adjustments though.

KPIs are typically just straight measurements and again, the emphasis is on managing performance of the ongoing business rather than linking to a defined improvement project. Formats can either be scorecards/dashboards, graphical, or a combination of both. It comes down to personal preference.

The important thing is that KPIs show a starting point (baseline), a target (eventual goal over some defined period), the intermediate values over time that will help the group get from baseline to target (plan), and of course the actual. KPI scorecards should also highlight exceptions visually, so you can move right to them in the discussion.

Figure 5.4 shows a KPI scorecard format illustrating the components mentioned. This is a scorecard for the month of December. Note that the scorecard shows a few historical months to show trend, and months into the future to illustrate the planned intermediate progress expected to reach the target. If you prefer a graphical approach, that's fine, I would just recommend also having the numerical scorecard as base data and for reference.

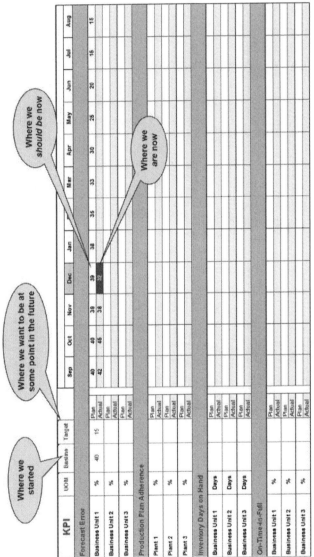

Figure 5.4 Sample KPI Scorecard

See the note in the Introduction for a link to download this spreadsheet.

Takeaways from Chapter 5 – Your Results Tracking Toolkit

- A set of tools will be required to manage all aspects of results management.
- The tools work together to manage definition, detailed calculation, summary visibility, and accountability.
- It can take 2-3 months to put this system in place, but once it's in place you'll be able to leverage the effectiveness of all components working together. They are all required and if you skip aspects of this, it will bite you at some point. You open yourself up to confusion and disagreement without the documented prior agreements to fall back on.
- The Results Tracker is used for focused improvement projects, whereas the KPI scorecard is used for the ongoing management of the business.

SIX

Managing Your Results
and Links to S&OP

We're nearing the end of this part of the story. Congratulations to those of you who made it through the details of Chapters 4 and 5. When you actually need to do it, you can go back and read the details more carefully. Like most jobs at the "make-it-happen" level, the devil is in the details and that's certainly the case with results management for S&OP and complex supply chain initiatives.

The higher-ups will often take this sort of thing for granted and some will never appreciate all that goes into it. They have to understand enough to sign-up for their benefits and resource their areas and tracking properly.

Executives are interested in the outputs though, and in some cases there may be a "hero or bum" mentality depending upon where the numbers are. I'm not sure there's a way around that, but there are some ways to spread the components associated with results management around, to ensure that the accountability for achieving results and the responsibilities for related tasks are put in the right places.

Don't go this results management thing entirely on your own, you'll need to have others engaged to get the required action especially when you hit bumps in the road, and like a country road after winter, they all have bumps.

Accountability for results throughout S&OP

As we can see, results management is a large effort for complex supply chain situations. It needs to have defined accountabilities and roles for various components. The accountability for actually achieving the results is of course the most important. As S&OP is a process comprised of different leaders, so too is a set of KPIs and corresponding result areas.

Result areas should be matched with the most appropriate executive who leads that section of the business and represents that part of the business in S&OP. These people could also make up a steering team in a dedicated project situation. If your project manager or lead is the one accountable for results, you probably won't get them and you're missing a key part of this book.

For example, if an increased sales benefit has been identified for the project and Marketing has been tasked with the development or improvement of a promotions management program, than a VP of Marketing would be a good choice to have accountability for the benefit. It's important that high levels in the company are accountable for the benefits.

The overall tracking and results management system should be initiated and standardized by a project manager level person. The specific tracking method for each benefit should be initiated by the functional lead/team member. It's the functional lead who develops the baseline and evaluation methodology, writes the corresponding document, then gets the relevant buy-in and signatures for their designated area.

In my world, that's typically a consultant who's paired up with a client functional lead. The consulting team should have been through this many times and should set the pace for all of this. There's a range of experience though, even across "experts". Project managers are in the background and can assist as required. As quickly as possible, tracking duties should be transferred to an impartial party that is reliable to compute benefits on the specified schedule.

Finance is typically best suited for this and it's a good idea to get those wheels in motion early. Not only by assigning resources, but also by ensuring that those resources are in the loop as the functional leads do their parts. As mentioned previously, finance should be involved in the construction of the central tracking tool.

If you skimp on resources here, you'll struggle with results management for the entire project and you likely won't be able to adjust to changing business conditions or effectively answer the questions from upper management. In my experience, a finance person in the 25 – 50% range should be sufficient. Sometimes there are a couple or few people split up among the benefit areas. Here's a summary of roles and responsibilities.

Executive leaders

- Accountable for the achievement of the results in the area(s) they own
- Allocates resources and provides guidance
- Understands baseline & evaluation methodologies for their area(s) and signs document
- Speaks to results status and takes corrective action when required
- One acts as the overall project sponsor

- Collectively form a steering team with the common goal of achieving the total benefits case

Project manager

- Provides standardized guidance and tools across functions/work areas
- Develops and implements centralized tools and templates
- Facilitates executive communication, prepares summary reports and presentations
- Enforces compliance with use of the tools and methodology
- Facilitates changes to baselines and benefit calculations to meeting changing business needs as required
- Works with finance to get their regular involvement
- Sees the whole results picture, integration points, and facilitates integration of interdependencies

Functional/area lead

- Completes the details related to tracking within their scope area, works with the project manager and their respective executive leader to manage results
- Work the details of any changes due to changing business conditions
- Responsible for delivering the benefits in respective area
- Complies with use of the results tracking system

Finance

- Takes over management of the results tracking tool
- Collects and/or certifies the values to populate tracking tools
- Traces recorded benefits to financial statements
- Works with area leads and the project manager on any adjustments that need to be made

Reporting results – Where should that occur and who should speak to results in review meetings?

Certainly not the most junior person in the room or a project manager. We need the higher-ups to own and talk about this. The last thing you want is a group of armchair generals who sit in meetings and pepper the underlings about gaps in their own areas.

The person that talks to the results and explains variance to plan should be the person accountable for them. The accountable executive will be much more into it if she has to present her results areas to her peer group.

I've been in many meetings where finance presents this information and explains any variances. Since they have no part in delivering these results, their presentations don't have much teeth, and everyone just yawns.

I think it's okay if finance presents a summary table or chart of results that they recorded (that will show that they "certified" the numbers), but it's important that the accountable executive lead discussions on successes as well as those explaining unfavorable variances.

Depending upon your situation you may create a project management structure for reporting and discussing project results (e.g. project and steering team meetings). This is a good way to go through project level progress (e.g. key progress and milestones, targeted training, integration points, issues) and have a wider participation from the people that are doing the work and are owners of the outputs.

The structure should normally consist of working and executive levels. The level of detail and conversation obviously needs to be tailored to each level. A dedicated project structure will take time and resources, but is often required to keep the focus on the project, especially during the early stages.

A way to avoid some overhead here may be to include this in the cycle of S&OP meetings. I'm not suggesting that we turn these meetings into project status meetings, but a tight summary of results status, gaps, issues, and celebrations could be worked into the meetings in combination with reviewing ongoing KPIs.

This could especially be appropriate for the executive meeting. We know how hard it is to get that group together and your project steering team should be most of members of the executive management team anyway. The sponsor and project manager should agree on the approach best for your situation.

Some result areas seem to be in conflict with one another

Well isn't that just supply chain for you! Isn't this what S&OP is supposed to resolve? Yes and yes. In some specific project situations, for whatever reasons (sometimes political ones), sometimes you'll have result areas that seem to be in direct conflict with each other. I've had it happen to me in my junior years when I was more of a consulting soldier.

An example of this might be minimizing unit cost or maximizing throughput in the plant while also reducing inventory. Another might be a headcount reduction situation, while reducing overtime on a tight parallel timeline. In this case, overtime could go up in the short run until the situation stabilizes and process improvements kick-in. If you're the sponsor or high in the organization you can just fix this or lead the team through it.

On the other hand, it may be planned this way because it's possible to get the right balance of progress in each of the seemingly conflicting areas, but the timing may not coincide as in the headcount/overtime example above. If you're low in the organization, you can certainly work with your sponsor on this. He or she may not do anything, it depends on what the situation is. I suggest you just press on and if there is a disconnect, make it visible at executive meetings.

At some point one of the executives will raise the issue, especially if it involves a benefit area in their area that falls behind. Sometimes it can be best to let an inconsistency go for a while, until someone in the right place decides to do something about it.

On-boarding your stakeholder group

As I've been talking about, it will take you a few cycles (months) to get your results tracking system up and running. During this time, you need to keep the subject of results visible. It will also

CASE STUDY – CONFLICTING BENEFITS

Early in my consulting career I was an area lead (or workstream lead as we call it) on a large improvement program for a large global company. There were actually two separate projects, one dealing with plant productivity across several plants, and the project I was on at headquarters which dealt with several things including supply chain. On the supply chain team, we had a large inventory benefit that we were struggling with. The plant project was substantially about increasing throughput and from our perspective, it seemed the plants weren't always building to demand. The company didn't have S&OP and it was even before I knew something called S&OP existed. We were primarily working in the sub-processes. For reasons I'll save for a personal conversation someday, our two projects had conflicting benefits and incentives on both the client and consulting sides.

One humid summer day in a southern US state, lightning struck the largest plant. No one was injured and it didn't do any serious damage, but it did take the plant down for a couple days. The plant teams lamented, while back it HQ it was high fives all around in the supply chain team room!

We didn't make the full inventory benefit, but we did get to some level of quasi-S&OP (more like structured common sense supply and demand discussions) to address these issues.

be necessary to educate your stakeholder team on your results tracking system.

They not only need to know about things like baselines and evaluation methodologies, but will also need to know terms such as cumulative and annualized. It's best to do this in one-on-one sessions with key stakeholders, and create a few summary slides for use in front of the whole group. You'll have to share these slides a few times as people get used to the terminology.

What to do after the project ends

Results tracking systems thankfully aren't meant to live forever. They're meant to be used to define and track results specific to focused efforts/projects. After the project ends, these tools are archived and the focus on results management shifts to the KPI scorecards.

Recall that for KPIs, the terms baseline, target, plan, and potentially forecast still apply. The baseline and evaluation methodology document is still important and the custody of these documents shifts to the functional leaders accountable for corresponding KPI performance.

Some best practices for S&OP KPI management

Here are some bullet points on S&OP KPI best practices that I use in training courses and with clients.

Table 6.1 KPI Management Best Practices	
Best Practice	**Comments**
S&OP KPIs link to high level business metrics above it and lower level execution metrics below it	▪ Think of a KPI tree structure and look for linkages, for example how do S&OP level metrics relate to business level metrics such as Return on Capital, or Revenue on one end, and maybe something more tactical like $/lb./mile or premium freight on the other end. Look for S&OP KPIs to be in the middle of company level and tactical KPIs.
You could have the same KPI in multiple S&OP meetings, but they would be at different levels for different audiences.	▪ For example in Demand Review, you may look at forecast error by sales territory or customer, but in Pre-S&OP you may look at it by product family or regionally, and in executive S&OP you may look at it at a company level.
KPIs have baseline & evaluation methodology documents	▪ Maintained by functional leaders
KPIs have reason codes for exceptions	▪ This is especially important for supply chain KPIs that involve multiple areas such as on-time-in-full or inventory turns ▪ Pareto analyses can be conducted on reason codes and determine where improvement effort should be focused
Root cause analysis should be completed on KPI exceptions	▪ Use the Pareto analyses as mentioned above and complete root cause analysis on the high occurrence reason codes ▪ Use fishbone diagrams and "5 Why Analysis" to find root causes of KPI exceptions ▪ Root cause analysis should not be conducted in the KPI review meeting, these are normally separate working sessions

Table 6.1 KPI Management Best Practices	
Review S&OP KPIs in the respective S&OP meetings	■ Map the system of KPIs to the system of S&OP meetings (e.g. demand-related KPIs in demand review) ■ Review quickly at the beginning of each meeting, focus on highlighted exceptions ■ Could share results of root cause analyses from prior working sessions ■ Record actions that address root causes of KPI exceptions
KPI Scorecard	■ Used more for on-going management of the business ■ Has a baseline, target, plan, and actual (could add forecast if the KPI is a budgeted item and you need to retain original plan) ■ Needs to be documented similar to project benefits ■ Numerical report supported by graphs ■ Highlights exceptions ■ Shows some history and the future plan

All of this really sounds like a lot

Baselining and evaluating, accountability for result areas spread around the executive team, results tracking tools, getting the data, a finance resource to track it, meetings to review…. oh boy, this all sounds like a lot. The truth is, it is a lot, especially to set it up.

Large change programs, requiring significant investment in internal resources, IT potentially, perhaps tens of millions in benefits at stake, and perhaps several million dollars in outside consulting fees require an ROI just like any other investment. Once the investment decision is made, results need to be tracked. Many teams don't have the wherewithal to pull it off as I've described, which will likely put them in the "no results" category for reasons described back in Table 2.1.

Lack of results management is one reason why so many change initiatives fail and one why so many S&OP processes flounder. Remember if you don't quantify and track specific benefits associated with the process and supply chain improvement, your stakeholders aren't really on the hook. You could lose them when they become distracted with the next fire that needs to be extinguished.

Take the steps one at a time. Determine what you need to improve, get some targets out there and obtain commitment at the right levels. Baseline your current state, write up the documents and get sign-offs, and start taking some measurements.

If something changes in the business that affects your numbers, work through it as you have to. Maybe it won't be an issue. The point is that you have to start somewhere. Over time you can refine your system as necessary, and your business cases for change will become even more compelling.

Recall the linkages back to S&OP

Recall our emphasis on how S&OP is the brain and skeleton that controls this body we call a company. It is the platform to make the company mind and body stronger. Use it as the framework for managing results in the business.

This means reviewing results related to dedicated improvement programs, managing KPIs throughout the meetings, integrating efforts, managing the trade-offs throughout the company, and aligning the focus of company leaders and their respective teams.

Depending upon your business, every month may not present a necessary executive level decision, and a weak process may cancel the executive meeting in that case. In addition to the need to confirm a go forward plan, every month does bring a need to review business results/KPIs. Thus a results-oriented process should never cancel this part of the executive meeting. Managing results through S&OP will keep this process front and center. Everybody who's anybody should want to be there.

Teams that aren't using S&OP, or aren't using it effectively to manage business results are falling behind at this point in the evolution of the competitive economy. Some will still succeed in spite of this, although underachieve what might have been possible, others will just lose relevancy in the face of real competition.

Most management teams I've worked with genuinely want the best company level outcome and have a whole company perspective (usually). They often just need to improve their process to illuminate the trade-offs necessary to make and implement the best decisions. When you are struggling to keep some leaders engaged in the process, focus on the outcomes, bring results into the discussion, and position S&OP as just the (necessary) means.

S&OP aligns and leverages human energy. When smart, hardworking, and determined people align and set their minds to something, human energy can become superhuman.

Takeaways from Chapter 6 – Managing Your Results and Links to S&OP

- Managing results has specific roles & responsibilities. They need to be defined and communicated.
- Finance can facilitate the communication of results, but executive owners need to speak to them publically.
- Some results areas may sometimes appear to be in conflict with one another, and these situations can be worked out through the process at the appropriate time.
- Use S&OP as the framework to manage business results and your executives will be engaged.
- Smart, hardworking, and determined people can be a formidable force when they work together.

Best in your improvement efforts.

About the Author

 Eric Tinker has spent the last 20 years in management consulting helping clients achieve large-scale change within their organizations. His projects thus far have resulted in over $500 million in operational improvements.

These results have been achieved through a combination of improving business processes, management systems and tools, information systems, organizational effectiveness, and by helping clients achieve sustainable behavioral change.

His client experience spans several countries and ranges from helping start-ups to leadership of large, complex, multi-geography business transformation. Eric focuses on S&OP and supply chain consulting change programs as well as training to help clients leverage S&OP to be the platform for continuous improvement in the organization. He has consulted and taught S&OP on 5 continents and works with a strong peer network of consultants and partner firms. His industry experience includes Consumer Goods, Energy, Chemicals, Life Sciences, and High Tech among others.

Prior to founding Nexview Consulting, Eric worked for organizations such as Celerant Consulting, Deloitte & Touche, Plan4Demand, and Hughes Aircraft. He has also worked as a freelance consultant with several other consulting firms. Eric is a CPA and holds a B.S. in Aerospace Engineering from Syracuse University, an M.S. in Mechanical Engineering from California

State University-Northridge, and an MBA from the University of Southern California.

In addition to helping clients be successful, Eric enjoys training, sharing content, and supporting/speaking at industry events. He has spoken at Institute of Business Forecasting, APICS, Institute for Supply Management, IE Group, and other public events as well as numerous private events.

Eric lives with his wife, son, and exuberant German shepherd in the woods of New Hampshire, but is also necessarily close enough to a good airport! Please feel free to contact him at ejt@nexviewconsulting.com or through the website.

Extras

Book Review Offer

I hope the book is helpful to you. As reviews can be very helpful to other potential readers, I'd like to offer you one of the Nexview supply chain best practice self-assessment toolkits free of charge in exchange for your review.

These toolkits are handy visual tools that survey several best practices and depending on responses, provide a visual indicator of strengths and development areas. We have them for S&OP, Demand Planning, Supply Planning, Distribution & Logistics, Procurement, and Upstream Oil & Gas. They are for sale on Nexview Online.

After your review is posted, just send a link to it in an email to info@nexviewconsulting.com, indicating which toolkit you'd like, and I'll send it to you.

Nexview Online

Nexview Online is a growing portal for S&OP and supply chain improvement content. We want to make it easy for people everywhere at all levels to have access to top consulting content and services that are generally only available through the traditional, high cost consulting model.

We have plans for various membership levels, but our free level provides access to our free content archive that has articles, blog posts, videos, survey results, conference presentations, and other items.

You can take a look at http://nexviewconsulting.com/join-us

Please feel free to reach me with any questions or comments at ejt@nexviewconsulting.com or through the website, and best in your improvement efforts!

21750648R00068

Printed in Great Britain
by Amazon